101 CREATIVE STRATEGIES FOR HELPING

Children with
HIGH
STRESS
Levels

A practical resource of
insights, approaches,
activities and
reproducible worksheets

(Pre-K – 8)

By: Donna Strom, Ed.S., L.P.C.
Brandie Rodgers, M.Ed.

© 2011, 2005 by
YouthLight, Inc.
Chapin, SC 29036

All rights reserved.
Permission is given for individual educators and counselors
to reproduce worksheets and activity pages only. Reproduction of these
materials for an entire school system is strictly prohibited.

Cover Design by Diane Florence
Layout/graphics by Elaine Callahan
Project Editing - Susan Bowman

ISBN 1889636894

Library of Congress
2005920818

10 9 8 7 6 5 4 3 2
Printed in the United States of America

P.O. Box 115
Chapin, South Carolina 29036
(800) 209-9774 • (803) 345-1070
Fax (803) 345-0888 • Email YL@sc.rr.com
www.youthlightbooks.com

Dedication

In loving memory of my momma, Bonnie Lynn Strom, whose example of faith even at the hardest times in life taught me how to deal with anxiety and stress.

In honor of my husband, Lang, who has been by my side during my most anxious and stressed times. I look forward to whatever the Lord has planned for the rest of our lives together.

Love,
Brandie

In honor of Ronald, who listens, encourages, strengthens, supports, worships with me, and helps me stay focused on the important things in life.

Love,
Donna

About the Authors

Brandie Rodgers lives in Ward, South Carolina with her husband, Lang. She holds a Master's Degree in Elementary Education with a focus on reading and literacy from Walden University and is a National Board Certified Teacher. She has been an elementary school teacher for eight years at Merriwether Elementary School in Edgefield County where she teaches 3rd grade.

Donna Forrest lives in North Augusta, South Carolina with her children Derek and April. She holds an Educational Specialist Degree in Counselor Education from the University of South Carolina. She is a Licensed Professional Counselor and National Board Certified Counselor. She has taught and been a school counselor at Merriwether Elementary School for 16 years and a therapist with the Center for Care and Counseling for 6 years.

Table of Contents

Understanding
HIGH STRESS
Levels in Children

© YouthLight, Inc.

Introduction

Thank you for your interest in helping children with high stress levels. It appears that the number of children exhibiting elevated stress levels is increasing. This book is intended to identify various roots of stress in children, the possible effects, some treatments, and proven interventions when working with these children.

Stress is normal in certain situations and can be considered either positive or negative. For example, a positive stress as a result of excitement might be a birthday party or an athletic event. A negative stress might be a result of a change in family situation, such as a divorce, or the rejection of a friend. While these feelings are uncomfortable, normal stresses must be handled almost daily. Children need to understand the meaning of stress in order to better equip themselves to handle this type of feeling. Some children experience anxiety and stress with change(s) such as a new school, new teacher, different friends, separation from a parent, tests, etc. By talking with a trusted person these feelings can be overcome.

When a child is unable to handle stress it can result in a problem that can lead to more serious effects. If it begins to last for longer periods of time and/or turn into panic or paranoia, then it may necessitate behavioral or cognitive interventions as directed by a counselor or doctor. It is important that these be addressed during the developmental stage in which they occur so that they do not become problematic for an entire lifetime.

Any adult who works with children (therapist, counselor, teacher, school administrator, parent, etc.) needs to be aware of several important factors:
- Children need to be educated on what are normal anxious feelings;
- Children need to be taught ways to cope with the stressors that lead to these feelings;
- Children need to identify and express specific current and past fears so clear coping mechanisms can be offered, practiced, and learned to deal with these stressors;
- Adults need to be aware of various developmental stages and milestones that account for ways children tend to respond to anxiety and stress; and,
- Adults need to be aware that anxiety and stress **can** be contagious so it is important that responses to children be as calm and consistent as possible.

This book addresses these factors, as well as when anxiety and stress become clinical problems that may need medical attention. Numerous strategies are offered to help children cope with various common types of anxieties that children today face. Many can be done individually, in small groups, or as classroom lessons. Resources for further study are available at the end of this book.

While there are no overnight fixes for most anxieties and stresses in children or adults, it is important that anyone experiencing these feelings realize ways to cope and continue in a normal routine as much as possible.

© YouthLight, Inc.

• *How are anxiety and stress evident in children?*

Anxiety and stress in children can be seen in a variety of ways. Some prevalent indicators for young children are excessive clinging to the caregiver, cannot sleep alone, or it may be difficult to be in a different room from parents. For school aged children some indicators are extreme shyness, timidness, clinginess, trouble getting along with other children, cannot go or stay asleep easily, more than one nightmare per week, complains often of headache and stomach ache, and they may have the need for a lot of reassurance. For adolescents, signs include over/under eating, excessive sleepiness, extreme concern over appearance, when severe at any age, can develop into phobias or panic attacks.

General symptoms of anxiety are shortness of breath, dizziness, a sinking feeling in the stomach, and accelerated heart beat (Schachter, 1988). At times, other physical symptoms may be present. Skin rashes, unexplained aches and pains, vomiting, or hyperactivity are examples of such physical symptoms. Always have those symptoms checked by a medical doctor first to rule out any physical problems.

Then, as will be discussed later in this book, educate and communicate with the child to help him/her cope with the stressors that are causing the discomfort. When children do not understand these feelings or how to cope with these feelings the anxiety and stress may turn into what appears to be sadness, tearfulness, anger, aggressiveness, or stubbornness. Children and adolescents may have one fearful situation that leads them to have unrealistic fears. The child then may appear hysterical with no logical explanation.

• *How do home and environment contribute to anxiety and stress in children?*

According to Steiner, "It is essential that you obtain a thorough family assessment that includes a family history of mood and anxiety disorders as well as the parents' typical responses to displays of anxiety or fear by the child. There is strong evidence suggesting that anxiety disorders may have a genetic component (Steiner, 1997)." Stressors that may lead to a child's anxiety that stem from the home environment can include marital conflict between parents, separation, or divorce. Arguing between parents can cause children to feel threatened or insecure. A child can restructure words overheard between parents during a minor disagreement to magnify into an unrealistic and frightening situation. When the arguments are more serious the child may become anxious about where he/she will live or with whom the child will live if the parents separate. At times the parent may turn to the child for support or sympathy, which can be destructive for the child who is unable to correct the problem. Children may become afraid to separate from either parent for fear they won't be there upon the return home. Divorce or separation is stressful. Children can feel they are to blame. They feel insecure that loyalties are being divided. It is important that the child is assured that he/she will not be abandoned and he/she is not to be blamed.

© YouthLight, Inc.

When a parent or loved one is ill, children can feel they are to blame. Children may feel they should be the one ill or, in extreme cases, feel they should die rather than the loved one. Parents should be calm, truthful and as factual as possible when children question about the illness without going into details that the child is not able to understand. Being open to discussion with the child is extremely important to minimize the anxiety and stress as much as possible.

Verbal ultimatums by parents can add anxiety and stress to children. Sometimes verbal comments may be internalized and misinterpreted by children as " I will never be good enough" or "I'm not worthy". Statements are sometimes made without thinking about the impact to a child or adolescent. Such statements as, "If you don't make an A on your report card, you won't be able to leave this house" becomes highly stressful to a sensitive child who is already truing to do his/her best. Or, "If your room isn't perfectly organized and straight when I get home from work, you will be on restriction!" is a statement that highly frustrates a hyperactive or unorganized child because their definition of "organized and straight" may not be the same as the parent who is giving the ultimatum.

Sibling rivalry often may be viewed as normal. However, children may find this a large source of stress within the home. The competitive and self confident nature of some children may enjoy the rivalry while other children may find this extremely stressful. Peer stress begins very early. A child may often realize at a young age that friends may be talented in areas that are not easy for him/her. Until that child is able to understand this is normal, anxiety and stress may be high.

Academic stress can begin as early as Kindergarten and heighten as the child progresses through the grades toward college and careers. For some children the grade of "50" might mean "I got half the answers right!" while for other children, the grade of "98" might mean "I missed two!"

A fear of being alone is a high stress factor for many children. For some this is a personality trait. For others it may be the result of constantly being around people without ever having realized that it is all right to play or be in a room alone. In more difficult cases, it may be the result of a trauma, such as an accident, death, or illness of a loved one.

Some other areas that cause children anxiety and stress are unfamiliar areas, severe weather, media coverage of horrible events, fires, thefts, and the list could continue. However, we do know that home and environment play a huge role in possible causing and well as ultimately helping a child with anxiety and stress.

© YouthLight, Inc.

© YouthLight, Inc.

• *What are some common anxiety disorders with children and adolescents?*

According to Frank, common anxiety disorders in kids include: panic disorder, phobias, separation anxiety disorder, obsessive-compulsive disorder, post-traumatic stress disorder, and generalized anxiety disorder (Frank, 2003). He states, "it is important to identify the type of anxiety disorder and treat it accordingly.

Panic Disorder entails severe and frightening times of strong fears and feeling of doom. These episodes may last anywhere from a few minutes to several hours. Chest pains, accelerated heartbeat, trouble breathing, fear of dying or losing control are all symptoms of a panic attack. When panic attacks are not treated and are experienced more frequently, the result may become a full Panic Disorder.

Phobias are described as a strong fear of a specific object or situation. A few common phobias are fear of animals, insects, storms, seeing blood, receiving injections, bridges, elevators, heights, and flying (Frank, 2003).

Separation Anxiety Disorder is described as great worry and stress concerning separation from the home or from those to whom a person is attached. A child experiencing this may refuse to sleep alone or go to school. The child may fear that an illness or accident will occur to a loved one or that he or she will get lost and not make it back to the loved one.

Obsessive-Compulsive Disorder deals with constant thinking, or obsessing, about specific things. These things may include germs, doing something wrong or bad, needing to put things in a particular order, or other worries or thoughts that cannot be put aside. The child may do things repetitively such as washing hands, ordering, double- checking, counting, or repeating words to themselves. These compulsions are done in an effort to reduce or terminate the stress and anxiety.

Post-Traumatic Stress Disorder is when a child continues to relive a terrifying event over a long period of time. The child may experience dreams or flashbacks that cause them to think the event is happening again. These symptoms may not surface until months after the event.

Generalized Anxiety Disorder is when the child worries more than normal every day for an extended period of time. The child may have trouble controlling the need to worry. Signs to look for with this disorder are: restlessness, edginess, over tiredness, lack of concentration, irritability, moodiness, and sleep disturbance.

• *What are some effects of childhood anxiety?*

Poor school attendance, lack of self-esteem, extreme and unwarranted fears, peer difficulties, deficit with interpersonal skills, alcohol abuse in teens, adjustment difficulties, and physical complaints are among some of the immediate complaints. While some anxieties come and go in children, the more serious can lead to anxiety disorders later if not recognized early.

• *What are some treatments available for anxiety disorders?*

Trained professionals (therapists, psychologists, school counselors, medical professionals) can offer various treatments. In his book, Turecki describes several forms of treatment that are available today. He explains that the approaches used today are "brief and practical" (Turecki, 1994). The list includes: psychodynamically-oriented long-term therapy, brief therapy, supportive therapy, play therapy, cognitive therapy, behavior therapy, group therapy, family therapy, adult therapy, parent guidance, and medication.

Hopefully, the goals of therapy will be met and therapy can end at that time. However, if there is very little or no progress after therapy he suggests that the situation be explored with the therapist to decide if therapy should continue. In his book, Martin points out that parents play a role in treatment as well. He says that "one of the most effective things you can do at home to help an anxious child is to really listen to and understand what he/she has to say" (Martin, 1995).

© YouthLight, Inc.

101

Creative Strategies and Suggestions

© YouthLight, Inc.

Introduction

This section is full of strategies and interventions to be used with individual children, small groups, and classrooms. There are creative examples, reproducible worksheets, lists, and questions for discussions throughout the section. We hope that teachers, counselors, and parents will find these to be quick and helpful references.

The *At-a-Glance* chart found on the following pages detail various ways to use each strategy. The (*) indicates the setting the strategy may be used (individual, small group, classroom), if a reproducible worksheet is available with that strategy, and the type of activity that is being used (visual, auditory, etc.).

Finally, there are *Tips for Parents* that support ways of helping the child learn to recognize and deal with stress.

© YouthLight, Inc.

At-a-Glance Chart — Uses for Each Strategy

#	NAME	INDIVIDUAL	SMALL GROUP	CLASSROOM	REPRODUCIBLE	VISUAL	AUDITORY	TACTILE	COGNITIVE	RELAXATION	PHYSICAL	PEER SUPPORT	HUMOR
1	Fear Factors!	*	*	*	*	*			*				
2	Time Table Keys	*				*							
3	Anxious But Not Alone	*				*							
4	Anxious Adjustments	*			*	*							
5	Loving Lunch Notes	*				*							
6	I'm Me....I'm Special	*	*	*	*	*							
7	Toning Down...		*	*	*	*	*						
8	Panic Points		*	*	*	*			*				
9	Agree to Disagree	*			*	*							
10	Hour Glass	*				*			*				
11	Night time Fun!	*				*		*					
12	Loving Links	*				*							
13	Tick Tock, Tick Tock	*				*		*					
14	Relaxing Reminders	*				*			*	*			
15	Picture Perfect	*	*			*							
16	Learn to speak your body's language	*	*		*	*		*	*				
17	Stress Signal					*							
18	Siesta Club		*				*			*			
19	I'm ALL That!	*	*				*						
20	I'm Scared!	*	*				*						

© YouthLight, Inc.

At-a-Glance Chart — Uses for Each Strategy

#	NAME	INDIVIDUAL	SMALL GROUP	CLASSROOM	REPRODUCIBLE	VISUAL	AUDITORY	TACTILE	COGNITIVE	RELAXATION	PHYSICAL	PEER SUPPORT	HUMOR
21	Relaxing Remedies			*			*		*				
22	Talking in Two's					*	*						
23	Jazzy Journal!	*					*		*				
24	Ring the Bell!!	*	*		*	*	*				*		
25	Imagine That!	*	*				*					*	
26	Punching Bag Rock!!		*	*			*						
27	RAP and RELAX (R&R)	*	*	*	*		*						
28	Wiggle and Giggle	*	*	*	*		*			*			
29	Mellowing Melodies	*		*			*						
30	Rollin', Rollin', Rollin'		*					*		*			
31	Critical Critters	*						*					
32	Handle That Job ONE Time!	*	*					*	*				
33	Pocket Protector	*						*					
34	Trying Transitions	*					*	*					
35	Calmness in Your Pocket...	*			*			*					
36	Squeeze Ball	*						*					
37	My Special Box	*				*		*	*				
38	Step it up!	*	*					*					
39	Let My Fingers Do the Walkin' and Talkin'!	*	*					*					
40	Finger Hugs!	*						*					

© YouthLight, Inc.

© YouthLight, Inc.

At-a-Glance Chart — Uses for Each Strategy

#	NAME	INDIVIDUAL	SMALL GROUP	CLASSROOM	REPRODUCIBLE	VISUAL	AUDITORY	TACTILE	COGNITIVE	RELAXATION	PHYSICAL	PEER SUPPORT	HUMOR
41	I've got ROCKS in my tummy!	*						*	*				
42	Clay Creations	*						*					
43	Stress Feelings – Action Chart	*	*		*	*			*				
44	Roll With The Word Punches!	*	*	*	*				*				
45	3 Pluses + A Wish			*					*				
46	Self Talk in Class	*							*				
47	Self Talk At Recess	*					*		*				
48	Interview for Another View!	*	*		*				*				
49	Tackle This Test!	*				*			*				
50	1st Things 1st!	*			*	*			*				
51	"You are never a loser until you quit trying."	*			*				*				
52	Recovering and Returning	*							*				
53	It's not WHAT you say …it's HOW you say it!	*	*		*	*			*				
54	Lovin' and Leavin'	*					*		*				
55	Miracle Pets!	*	*		*				*				
56	Checking The Mind	*							*				
57	My Teacher and Me	*							*				
58	Different or Better???	*							*				
59	Name that Attention!	*			*				*				
60	Change can be FUN!	*							*				

At-a-Glance Chart — Uses for Each Strategy

#	NAME	INDIVIDUAL	SMALL GROUP	CLASSROOM	REPRODUCIBLE	VISUAL	AUDITORY	TACTILE	COGNITIVE	RELAXATION	PHYSICAL	PEER SUPPORT	HUMOR
61	F.L.Y. (FIND ways to LOVE YOURSELF)	*	*		*				*				
62	A.D.H.D.'s. (Attitude Does Help Determine Success!)	*	*	*					*				
63	Program My Brain!	*	*		*				*				
64	Smart Starts!	*		*					*				
65	Table Time	*							*				
66	Book of Blessings	*						*	*				
67	Repeat, Repeat, Repeat	*							*	*			
68	Delegate Duties	*	*						*				
69	Recognize Reactions	*							*				
70	Food Facts	*						*	*				
71	Who am I?	*	*	*	*				*				
72	Get Focused	*							*				
73	Lighten the Load	*							*				
74	Prescription For Rest	*			*					*			
75	Get your Zzzzzz's	*								*			
76	Peaceful Place	*								*			
77	Work Out Wonders	*								*			
78	Calming Collages	*								*			
79	Stress OR Stretch!	*	*	*							*		
80	I Don't Feel Too Good!	*								*	*		

© YouthLight, Inc.

© YouthLight, Inc.

At-a-Glance Chart — Uses for Each Strategy

#	NAME	INDIVIDUAL	SMALL GROUP	CLASSROOM	REPRODUCIBLE	VISUAL	AUDITORY	TACTILE	COGNITIVE	RELAXATION	PHYSICAL	PEER SUPPORT	HUMOR
81	Lap it UP!	*									*		
82	Crossover (physical exercise)!	*	*	*							*		
83	Jelly Belly	*								*	*		
84	Big Brother/Big Sister	*										*	
85	Study Buddies		*	*								*	
86	OK Opinions		*									*	
87	Scavenger Hunt!		*									*	
88	Newcomer's Club		*									*	
89	Unique Expressions		*		*							*	
90	The Smile Challenge!	*	*	*								*	*
91	The FRIEND game!			*								*	
92	Friendly Facts	*										*	
93	Babbling Benefits	*										*	
94	Healthy and Wise!		*									*	
95	Merry Mistakes!	*	*										*
96	Learn to Laugh			*									*
97	Shout and Squeal!		*										*
98	Scream Sack	*	*										*
99	Laughing Bag!	*											*
100	Stress Cards!		*										*
101	Tips for Parents	*											

Introduction

There are several advantages to using visual strategies with children. These strategies allow the child to visualize what is being discussed. For many children seeing something in print, a picture, a chart, or a list enables them to remember better.

STRATEGY #1
Fear Factors!

Common school fears include separating from a caregiver, test taking, tone of teacher's voice, large or different building, peer interactions, bullies, etc. Use the following "Fear Factor!" worksheet during individual, small group, and classroom lessons to identify and discuss the realities of such fears versus irrational thoughts. Have each child complete columns 1-4. Complete column 5 together after talking through the fear.

© YouthLight, Inc.

© Youthlight, Inc.

1 FEAR FACTOR! What makes you feel afraid?	**2** Date of 1st Fear. When did you start having this fear?	**3** Who/What can help?	**4** What is the worst thing that could happen?	**5** What have I learned from this discussion?

FEAR FACTOR WORKSHEET

STRATEGY #2
Time Table Keys

Anxiety sometimes heightens when a time schedule must be met. This could be a project that is due at school, a timed math test, a homework assignment that must be done before leaving for ball practice, or getting up on time in the mornings. Use these keys to help teach the child how to reduce his/her anxiety when working to meet deadlines.

• Write in a planner due dates and schedule small segments of the work to do daily.

Draw a **#1** in the date for the beginning stage.

A **#2** with a smile for the middle stage date.

A **#3** on the date to finalize.

• On timed tests draw a line in the middle. Decide when half the time is up and use this as a visual aid. Only work with the problem in front of you and set a time limit to move on if you haven't arrived at an answer (you can skip that problem and return to it later);

• Draw two clocks (12") – a YELLOW one that shows the time 10 minutes early (beside bed) and a GREEN one that shows 5 minutes early (on the other side of the room). Actually set 2 real alarm clocks beside each (the yellow and green) to go off at these times. The visual clocks that were drawn are immediate reminders that it is important to wake up now!

Point out the KEYs to any scheduled or timed event is PLANNING!

September						
Sun	Mon	Tue	Wed	Thu	Fri	Sat
	#1	2	3	4	5	6
7	#2	9	10	11	12	13
14	#3	16	17	18	19	20
21	22	23	24	25	26	27
28	29	30				

© YouthLight, Inc.

STRATEGY #3
Anxious But Not Alone

Often a child may obtain a sense of peace by learning that everyone has feelings of anxiety from time to time. Have the child(ren) write a letter to someone they love or to a famous person asking that person to share a story about something that has made them anxious. Also, ask how have you handled it? Draw a picture for that child(ren) showing the situation. Invite the child(ren) to share what is causing them to feel anxiety and allow them to identify ways he/she can change the way he/she reacts. Have the child(ren) draw a "before" picture showing when and how the anxiety was felt and a "after" picture showing how the reaction can reduce the stress.

STRATEGY #4
Anxious Adjustments

When a child has difficulty adjusting to change, routine is extremely important. This activity requires the school and parent(s) working together to set up a calendar (preferably for one month at a time). Visually, the child can see the routine and check off daily activities. This helps him/her understand that the "routine" includes various daily activities rather than separating week-ends from week days. An example of such as calendar is shown below (for a 1 week period

SUNDAY	MONDAY	TUESDAY	WEDNESDAY	THURSDAY	FRIDAY	SATURDAY
Family Time	**7:45-3:00** School **3:00-4:00** Errands **4:00-5:00** Play time **5:00-6:00** Homework **6:00-7:00** Dinner **7:00 to bedtime** Relax	**7:45-3:00** School **3:00-4:00** Errands **4:00-5:00** Play time **5:00-6:00** Homework **6:00-7:00** Dinner **7:00 to bedtime** Relax	**7:45-3:00** School **3:00-4:00** Errands **4:00-5:00** Play time **5:00-6:00** Homework **6:00-7:00** Dinner **7:00 to bedtime** Relax	**7:45-3:00** School **3:00-4:00** Errands **4:00-5:00** Play time **5:00-6:00** Homework **6:00-7:00** Dinner **7:00 to bedtime** Relax	**7:45-3:00** School **3:00-4:00** Errands **4:00-5:00** Play time **5:00-6:00** Homework **6:00-7:00** Dinner **7:00 to bedtime** Relax	**Morning:** Chores (i.e. clean room, etc.) & play time **Afternoon & Evening:** Family & Friends Time

© YouthLight, Inc.

ACTIVITY SHEET

SUNDAY	MONDAY	TUESDAY	WEDNESDAY	THURSDAY	FRIDAY	SATURDAY

© YouthLight, Inc.

STRATEGY #5
Loving Lunch Notes

For anxious or oversensitive children, lunch is a great time to be reminded that someone from home is thinking of them. Jot down a quick visual reminder to your child and place it inside their lunchbox or lunch money envelope. Your message can be inspirational such as "I can't wait to see you after school" or "I love you so much – have a great day!" The message can also be motivational. For example, "Remember – you can do anything you put your mind to" or "You never know what you can do until you try." A good message on a test day may be "You studied hard all week – I know you'll do great on your test today!"

STRATEGY #6
I'm Me…I'm Special

Sibling comparisons can often be a source of stress for children. Use this strategy to teach children that everyone is different and that is what makes us special. This activity can be used at home or at school. Have children complete the activity sheet titled "Who am I?" or "Spotlight on Me!" The sheet will list several questions for the children to draw (and color) such as: favorite book, subject, pet, food, hobby, TV show, animal, place, song, sport, movie, as well as questions such as: I'm good at…, When I grow up I want to be a… Have the children draw a self-portrait and display these with the activity sheet. Show the children how being different can allow them to help others. For instance, if a child is good at math they could offer to help someone who struggles in that area. If the child wants to become a better baseball player they could as someone for help who listed baseball as their favorite sport. (See the following worksheet.)

© YouthLight, Inc.

WHO AM I?

A picture of my favorite book .....

A picture of my favorite subject in school...

A picture of my favorite pet...

A picture of my favorite hobby....

A picture of my favorite TV show (or DVD)...

* A picture of ME ...

© YouthLight, Inc.

ACTIVITY SHEET

STRATEGY #7
Toning Down ...

Children who are over anxious or stressed often respond better to softer tones of voice. In a classroom or small group give each child a copy of the worksheet with the stoplights. Allow the children to color the circles and discuss the meaning of each. The **green** color is where you want to be (normal tone), the **yellow** is a warning that you may be getting too loud or harsh, and the **red** signals that you need to stop and cool down. Being aware of your tone is key when helping children feel safe and secure when they are around you.

Then play a game stating the following statements. Have the students point to the correct color on their stop light.
Practice – Teacher:
• (Normal tone – GREEN) "Please stand up beside your chair."
• (Warning tone – YELLOW) "Get out of that chair now."
• (Stop, cool down tone – RED) "GET OUT of that chair NOW!"

Continue letting the children respond to these statements varying your voice tone:
• GIVE ME THAT PENCIL! (RED)
• Please go get the ball for me. (GREEN)
• Give me that book now! (YELLOW)
• Thank you for that pencil. (GREEN)

Allow children to discuss how the different voice tones make them feel. Now allow them to practice with the group and you restate their sentences using a different tone. (Example: If their tone is loud, you restate the sentence using a softer tone.) Finally, allow the children to discuss that "loud" voices are not necessarily something to be afraid of, but sometimes are used to get immediate attention.

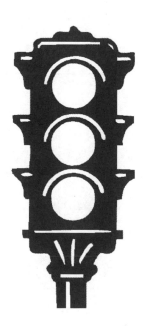

© YouthLight, Inc.

TONING DOWN WORKSHEET

STATEMENT	COLOR (TONE)	HOW COULD MY TONE BE BETTER
GIVE ME THAT PENCIL!		
Please go get the ball for me.		
Give me that book NOW!		
Thank you for helping.		

© YouthLight, Inc.

STRATEGY #8
Panic Points

Common stressors or panic points often go unnoticed and unidentified. In order to deal with them properly, children need to be able to identify these panic points. Lead a discussion having children name some "panic points" (example – timed tests, dark rooms, etc.) Record this brainstormed list on chart paper or the chalkboard.

Next, give each child the following worksheet that lists many stressors that children face in everyday life. Allow the children to privately complete the checklist. Leave space at the bottom for the child to write in any panic points he/she may experience that aren't listed. If working with a group of children, allow discussion of panic points each child is willing to share. Monitor closely and follow up with those who indicate more serious fears. Then fill in the pyramid for a personal visual!

© YouthLight, Inc.

SITUATION	MILD PANIC	MEDIUM PANIC	EXTREME PANIC
Being picked on or bullied			
Being late to school or class			
Not getting picked to be on a team			
Feeling bad			
Arguing with a friend			
Not having school supplies			
Tests			
Parents arguing			
Sisters/Brothers arguing			
Not enough time to finish			
Losing a game			
Dark rooms			
Being alone			

© YouthLight, Inc.

MILD PANIC

MEDIUM PANIC
(some stress most days)

EXTREME PANIC(the most stress)

© YouthLight, Inc.

STRATEGY #9
Agree to Disagree

When parents argue, many times the child becomes afraid and anxious. This activity will help the child learn that it is all right to "agree to disagree."

The parent or counselor or teacher should allow the child to draw or list 3 ways he/she disagrees with his/her parent. Write these on the top 1/3 of the paper by the sad face. Next, the child will draw or list 3 ways he/she agrees or enjoys his/her parent by the happy face. Finally, ask the child how he/she feels about his/her parent(s) (i.e., love, think they are fun, etc.). Then lead a discussion of how we can "love and live" with someone, but not always "like or agree" with that person's actions. By having the child lead this activity, follow up with a discussion that parents (and friends) can love each other and still disagree also. Draw or list those in the column under the hands!

© YouthLight, Inc.

© YouthLight, Inc.

STRATEGY #10
Hour Glass

Using an hour glass, talk with the child about the length of time it will take for the sand to fill the empty side. Compare that time with a time frame in which the child is familiar. Then have the child tell about his/her current fears while the hour glass begins to fill. Allow the child to draw a picture of the "worst" thing that could result from those fears and discuss the real thoughts versus the unreal fears. After no longer than 15 minutes begin changing the focus by discussing plans later in the hour, day, or week. Focus on good plans or goals and how the child can get to this point of time. Note the sand passing through the hour glass and point out that even with the greatest fear…"This too shall pass!"

STRATEGY #11
Night Time Fun!

When a young child struggles with dark rooms or sleeping alone, have objects in the room to "guard" him/her. These can be stuffed animals strategically placed (at the door, window, beside the bed, etc.). Before going to bed structure a game with the child and parent talking to each animal and giving them their assignment for the night. For example, "Mr. Bear, you are big and tough. When you sit in my window, we know that you will let me know if someone tries to come in because you will fall on the floor and I will hear! Thanks for guarding the window." Or for the stuffed puppy on the bed with the child, "Pooch, if I get lonesome, I know you will be right here to hug me and remind me that I'm not alone." This can be a fun ritual that a child looks forward to even when they have passed the initial fears (and one they will remember forever!)

© YouthLight, Inc.

STRATEGY #12
Loving Links

Being left in the care of others, whether it's child-care or school, can be stressful for many children. It can be a rough transition for child and parent when the child must leave the parents arms and go to another's. There are things a parent can do however to make this a little easier. The idea here is to link both worlds for the child. Allowing the child to bring a favorite toy or picture of Mom and Dad is one way to do this. Another approach is to build a strong relationship with the caregiver. Let your child see you talking with the teacher or sitter and asking about what went on during the day. They will receive comfort knowing that you are involved and are aware of what goes on during the day. Also, dropping by during the day when possible to see your child or share a lunch with them reinforces your involvement. Some children also benefit from seeing where Mom or Dad work each day. This is another link to you and your world that the child can connect to.

STRATEGY #13
Tick Tock, Tick Tock

Many children need help learning how to manage their time. Children today are involved in many activities at an early age. It can be hard to juggle school assignment, sports practice, church groups, and after school activities such as clubs. Even young children can benefit from learning how to use a planner or calendar. Provide your child with some type of daily organizer. It could be an assignment book for school that has a page for each day, a copy of a monthly calendar, or a weekly planner. Help your child fill in dates using symbols or pictures cut out of magazines indicating athletic (piano, dance, etc.) practices, meetings, and due dates for school-work. Work together to set deadlines for getting assignments done ahead of time and fill those in. This can help children learn how to use their time wisely and plan ahead. This will alleviate a lot of stress for the busy child!

© YouthLight, Inc.

STRATEGY #14
Relaxing Reminders

Pictures are wonderful reminders of those we love. This activity would use actual photographs or symbols to remind the child of people and ways that are relaxing to them. For example, a picture of the child playing with a friend or a parent, a photo of a special stuffed animal, a picture of their home, or a picture of a favorite pet. This could be placed in the front of a notebook cover, on a piece of paper (laminated) to be kept in his/her school desk, or placed on his/her cubby in the classroom as a reminder of relaxing moments that will be experienced after school!

As an alternative to this activity, the child could use the pictures below to write or draw his/her feelings about relaxing with something in the photograph!

© YouthLight, Inc.

© YouthLight, Inc.

STRATEGY #15
Picture Perfect

Help children learn how to picture themselves in their favorite place. This can be a very calming exercise. Work with the child to think of the one place where they feel the safest. It may be their bedroom, at a loved one's house, in a tree house, etc. The child can learn to picture this place in their mind in order to relieve stress or anxiety. They could also illustrate this place and keep the picture with them to look at during the day.

STRATEGY #16
Learn to speak your body's language

Everyone's body has its own language. Work with children to look at their body in order to understand what they are feeling. When a child is over anxious or sensitive have them complete the body language worksheet to identify what signals their body is giving off. This can be a tool to help them learn how to relax by identifying the signs of stress.

© YouthLight, Inc.

 Look in a mirror – what do your eyes look like now? Draw them.

 What is your facial expression? Draw it.

 What is the position of your shoulders and arms? Draw them.

Now illustrate what you would like for your body language to show. (relaxed eyebrows, smile, relaxed facial muscles, straight back and relaxed arms)

BODY LANGUAGE WORKSHEET

© YouthLight, Inc.

STRATEGY #17
Stress Signal

Discuss the three levels of anxiety. Then have the child DRAW and explain why this makes him/her feel anxious. Brainstorm and write beside the drawing things to do to reduce the stress.

1) **Mild** – These are anxious feelings that you think about briefly but don't worry over a long period of time.
For example, you are playing in a baseball game and are a little nervous that you might not do well. However, when you step up to bat and try, the nervousness goes away quickly.

2) **Medium** – These are anxious or stressful feelings that might keep you awake some nights or that you think about during the day, but you are able to sleep some or go about the regular duties of the day.
For example, you don't like leaving your mom when you go to school in the mornings. But you walk into the school building and soon begin to enjoy your day. The anxious feelings might return the next night, but you are able to continue going to school.

3) **Severe** – These are stressful feelings that keep you from participating in an activity.
For example, panic over leaving your parent(s) before school but yet you know your teacher loves you and helps you. However, you find yourself crying each morning before school.

© YouthLight, Inc.

Introduction

The following auditory strategies will be beneficial for children who prefer to use their sense of hearing to process data by hearing. These activities offer music, rhythm, voice tone, and rap ideas. A sense of fun, excitement and relaxation can be obtained through sounds.

STRATEGY #18
Siesta Club

Rest is very helpful when struggling with anxiety, but is sometimes very hard to do when anxious feelings are prevalent. In a small group with anxious children, have them relax to soft music the first 10 minutes of the meeting. Then gradually turn the music down and in a calm voice begin the group. That first 10 minutes of rest can show the children how relaxation can assist with anxious or stressful feelings. Help the children think of ways to translate the "siesta" time to help with identified "anxious" or "stressful" times.

STRATEGY #19
I'm ALL That!

This activity is designed to help the child develop confidence and have fun at the same time which can greatly reduce anxiety symptoms.
1. Have the child name one activity that he/she excels in and describe feelings he/she experiences when doing that activity.
2. Then, ask him/her to pat himself/herself on the back while saying in a **normal tone** of voice, "I'm ALL that!"
3. Next, have the child name something that his/her parent or grandparent says that is good about them.
4. Repeat #2 in a **stronger** voice.
5. Have the child tell about a time he/she helped someone else do something good.
6. Repeat #2 in a **loud** voice.
7. Continue with positive statements about the child and repeating #2 until it becomes similar to a cheer!
8. Finally, discuss how positive feelings lead to happy results, so when anxious thoughts come (including fears) try to remember some positive thoughts to balance and help one feel better!

© YouthLight, Inc.

STRATEGY #20
I'm Scared!

The definition of "scared" varies for children. Often a loud voice, an active teacher who moves around the room a lot, frequent laughter, or firmness can be interpreted to a child as "scary." In this activity the counselor encourages the child(ren) to name the things about an adult that "scares" him/her. Of course, physical aggressiveness would not be included in this activity.

If the child says, "My teacher yells all the time," have the child tell how this has made him/her scared. In general, it's the thought more than the action. Then, the counselor, using fluctuations in his/her voice, speak loudly and softly but show how the words are the same but the tone different.

> (Example) LOUD "I'm going to close the door now!"
> SOFT "I'm going to close the door now."

Have the child describe and compare his/her feelings with those two tones. Continue with naming some opposites to compare. For example, happy versus mad face or hands on hips versus pointing fingers toward someone or walking calmly toward you while talking softly versus walking fast with a loud voice.

© YouthLight, Inc.

STRATEGY #21
Relaxing Remedies

Offer these suggestions to the teacher if a child is reporting anxiety and stress within the classroom.

• Have soft, instrumental or nature sounds played continuously in the classroom during written assignments or reading times;

• Check voice tones of all – teachers and peers – and implement a "fun rule" to help keep those tones in check (i.e. If a child (or teacher) gets loud, have them place a mark on the board under the word "Ouch!" After each day, if there are no marks, the class gets a bonus of the teacher's choosing.

• Breathe deep exercise as a class between subjects and/or assignments (children love this!);

• Stretch and whisper for 3 minutes between subjects and/or assignments

STRATEGY #22
Talking in Two's

Being asked to relay messages between two people who are angry with each other can be stressful for the messenger. An example of this sometimes occurs when parents are separated or divorced. A child may be asked to, "Go tell your father…" by the mother. Or, with friends, one friend may direct a child to go tell another friend, "She doesn't want to play with you anymore." The child may feel pulled between the two people.

It is important that we give the child strategies to pull out of the triangle of three.

© YouthLight, Inc.

Directions: Label each corner of the triangle with a name (be sure to include your own). Tell about a time you got into an argument with one of those people named on the corner of the triangle and explain what actually happened. Then brainstorm with your counselor (or other children in the group) how you could handle this with one person at a time – or better yet – how you could move out of the triangle and let the other two people settle the disagreement if it was a disagreement that you were not involved in at the start.

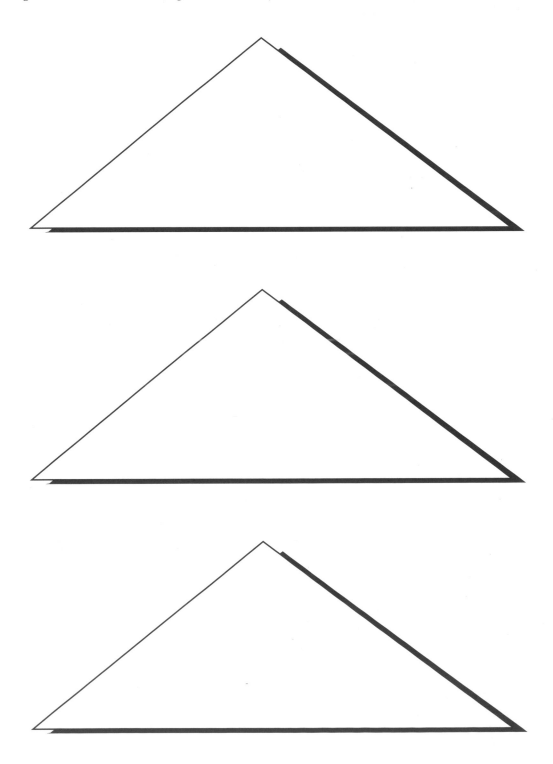

© YouthLight, Inc.

STRATEGY #23
Jazzy Journal!

Using an upbeat, instrumental tune (great from movies or cartoons), have the child verbally (or written) identify things that make him/her happy and relaxed. These can be things at home or school. Either the child, parent, or counselor can record these good feelings and activities. Then, turn the music off and make up an original upbeat tune to sing those! Record this on an audio tape and have the child play this when he/she feels anxious.

STRATEGY #24
Ring the Bell!
(Great for children who have difficulty verbalizing their feelings.)

Often anxious children are very serious thinkers. Sometimes appropriate humor can relieve stress and anxiety. Either individually or in a small group set up a format similar to a TV game show. The caller (counselor, parent, or teacher) will name good feelings and feelings that appear to cause anxiety in the child. The child will be given a small bell with instructions to stay silent on the good, peaceful feeling statements and ring the bell for 3-5 seconds on the anxious or disturbing feeling statements. When the child rings the bell the caller will respond with a jump, fearful look, etc. which usually results in the child laughing. Then discuss the real versus imagined parts of that anxious feeling.

© YouthLight, Inc.

- Listening to the ocean

- Yelling

- Loud music

- Forgetting my chores

- Bad hair day

- Sudden loud noises

- Crawling on the sofa to watch TV

- Soft singing

- Sleeping late on Saturday morning

- Leaving home when I come to school

- Getting up after not much sleep

- Coming to school to take a test, but didn't have time to study

- Friend is mad at me

- Getting into trouble in class with the teacher

- Afraid I'll make a mistake (where?)

© YouthLight, Inc.

STRATEGY #25
Imagine That!

Ask the child(ren) to close their eyes. Have soft music in the background. Calmly have the child talk about their most pleasant thought of a loved one or pet. Encourage the child to verbalize a description of that person/pet. Have the child describe how this person looks, what they enjoy doing together, feelings (i.e., of safety, comfort, etc.) and then talk about when they will see that person/pet again. What are you plans? Will you do the same fun things or something different? After this discussion, talk about how there can be pleasant thoughts that follow stressful situations. These thoughts can help get through the more anxious feelings.

STRATEGY #26
Punching Bag Rock!!!!!

This is a great group activity! Get a "squeeze ball" and have each child write on a strip of paper something that makes him/her anxious (NO names on the papers). While the music is plays in the background allow the child to tape the strip of paper to the squeeze ball and "punch it out" (several times each). When each child has completed this, the leader should turn the music off and read some of the anxious thoughts from the strips of papers. Then allow the class (or small group) to discuss each of those thoughts. The children feel safe in this activity because none are singled out individually and good ideas for overcoming those anxious feelings are given by peers!

STRATEGY #27
RAP and RELAX (R & R)!

Using the "Rap" on page 42, help the child(ren) learn and perform (for another group or class). Then discuss ways to relax after enjoying the "Rap."

© YouthLight, Inc.

RAP and RELAX (R & R)!

ACTIVITY SHEET

When you're really uptight
    And all stressed out,
It's not much help
    To cry or to pout.

But if you truly
    Want to relax,
Smile really, really big
    And learn these facts!

First, of all
    You must learn to trust
And talk to someone soon
    Or you will bust!

For there are some fears
    That are very real,
But, then there are others
    That only you feel.

So, take this advice
    In your head and heart
Talking to someone
    Is a real good start!

© YouthLight, Inc.

STRATEGY #28
Wiggle and Giggle....

Laughter can be one of the best medicines! Sing and act out with the child(ren) the song "If You're Happy and You Know It ... (shake your hand, shake your foot, nod your head, laugh a lot, etc.) Act out each verse and the result will be some smiles and laughter! Refer to the words on Page 44 for the final verse and repeat as many times as the child(ren) wish!

© YouthLight, Inc.

ACTIVITY SHEET

Wiggle and Giggle....

If you're happy and you know it
Wiggle and giggle!

If you're happy and you know it
Wiggle and giggle!

If you're happy and you know it,
then your face will really show it,
If you're happy and know it
Wiggle and giggle!

© YouthLight, Inc.

STRATEGY #29
Mellowing Melodies

Listening to the right type of music can be very soothing for children. There are many varieties of soothing sounds sold on CD's today. Classical music, rain showers, beach waves, nature noises, etc. can be purchased. Sound machines are also on the market which play sounds such as a heartbeat, animals sounds (birds, crickets, frogs), etc. Let your child listen to several types and decide which is the most soothing to him/her. In school, you may keep these selections in the listening center. At home, let the child have access to a CD player or sound machine to use when they need to sooth themselves.

© YouthLight, Inc.

Introduction

Various levels and intensities of touch can provide important comfort and remind children when stress is being experienced. Tactile approaches will emphasize real feelings and thoughts through touch.

STRATEGY #30
Rollin', Rollin', Rollin'

Action and discussion are important to reducing anxiety and stress in children. A bowling game can be constructed using 10 plastic bottles and a small soccer ball (or the Physical Education teacher may loan a real children's bowling game). Each child will name one fear that exists at school. That child will then attempt to knock down the plastic pins (bottles) after naming one strategy that might help overcome that fear. After three tries the next child repeats the activity. Each pin down counts as one point. The first child to get to thirty (30) points wins!

STRATEGY #31
Critical Critters

Children often need to be taught how to take criticism and learn from it. Using puppets in a role play can help children see that criticism isn't always a bad thing. Using one-to-one instruction the adult can be the first to respond to the criticism offered by the child's puppet. For instance, "It was obvious in PE today that you don't know anything about basketball" – "I've never played much – would you help me today at recess?"

© YouthLight, Inc.

STRATEGY #32
Handle That Job ONE Time!

It has been said that to organize a room or office area, papers should be handled ONE time. In other words, put in the right place the first time and they are not handled repeatedly.

This concept can be used in this activity with children. Have them name things they do not like to do or they feel pressured for time. The counselor might want to ask them to name some time recently they had to search or hunt for a pencil, a homework paper, a shoe, etc.! Then discuss and practice how they can put it in the right place the first time by taking an extra few seconds and time is not wasted or frustration is not reached when they cannot find the items later!

STRATEGY #33
Pocket Protector

For small children, leaving a safe home to go to school can cause anxiety. One strategy to use with these children is to provide them with a small token that can stay in their pocket during the day. This could be a small picture of a loved one, a little note, a special stone, rock, marble, or coin.

© YouthLight, Inc.

STRATEGY #34

Trying Transitions

(For the child transitioning between mom and dad's homes)

When the child returns from a week-end with a parent to his/her primary home, sometimes the child is anxious about the change in general. This carries over to school and peer interactions. The parent and teacher can help with this adjustment period by pre-planning several "transition activities." Some examples of these to be done after each transition could be:

- Write the parent (household just left) a note talking about the visit and have the parent (primary household) mail that letter. This indicates to the child both parents are OK with the feelings of adjustment the child is experiencing.
- Make an audio tape to send to the absent parent talking about the previous (or next planned) visit.
- Allow the child time to talk about the visit and identify feelings of sadness, insecurity, etc. Be sure to offset these feelings by having the child identify positive feelings, good memories, etc.

STRATEGY #35

Calmness in Your Pocket ...

Have the child discuss the "soft" and comfortable feeling of the cotton ball in the felt as compared to the "hard" and uncomfortable feeling of the pebble (marble) in the other piece of felt.

Allow the child to keep it in his/her pocket or school desk to touch when feeling anxious or stressed.

© YouthLight, Inc.

Calmness in Your Pocket ...

Instructions:

- Cut two pieces of felt 2" X 2." You will need a needle with a 16" piece of thread that matches the felt, 2 cotton balls, and a small pebble (or marble).
- With one piece of felt fold in half (1" X 2" size) and put the 2 cotton balls inside. Sew near the edge by hand so the cotton balls are secure inside the felt.
- With the other piece of felt, follow the instructions above, except put the pebble (or marble) inside and sew the edges together.

1. CUT 2 felt pieces

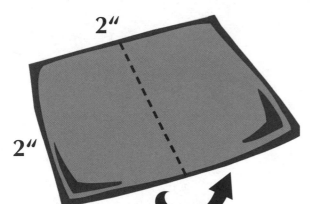

2. FOLD each in half

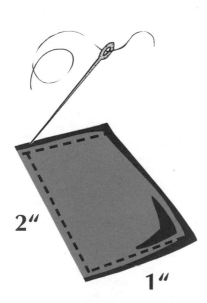

3. ADD cotton balls

4. ADD marble/rock

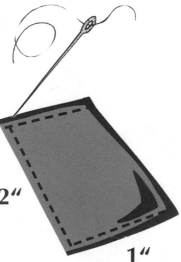

5. SEW each folded piece all the way around

© YouthLight, Inc.

STRATEGY #36
Squeeze Ball

This activity allows the child to MAKE a "Squeeze Ball" that can be carried in his/her pocket. Using a funnel and baking soda, fill the balloon and tie the end (two would be even better – one for each hand). Then, when stress or anxiety is highest, squeeze the balloon as a reminder that stress tightens body muscles and squeezing tires the same muscles which serves as a physical release that can be done sitting or standing, walking or running!

STRATEGY #37
My Special Box

Ask the child to write (or tell if they are younger) every thought that is stressful to them currently. Then take the piece of paper and put it in a small box. Help the child wrap the box with pretty wrapping paper and tie it with a bow. Talk about how the concerns and stresses are "all wrapped up" and allow the child to give the box to a special caretaker. (parent, grandparent, teacher, counselor, etc.) Then talk to the child about allowing that caretaker to "handle worrying" while the child continues with his/her day. This activity works well with visual and kinesthetic learners.

© YouthLight, Inc.

STRATEGY #38
Step it up!

This activity is best to do outside on a playground or area with dirt. Take a stick and draw in the dirt 5 "steps." Number the steps from bottom to top. Then talk about the following as the child puts his/her foot in each step as it is being discussed.

Step #1: Name that worry!
Step #2: Identify one way you have already tried to get over that worry.
Step #3: Think of one new way you can try to feel less anxiety.
Step #4: Talk about how your attitude can help (i.e. smiling, etc.).
Step #5: Decide how to "step over the worries" with your positive (good) attitude and DO IT!

STRATEGY #39
Let My Fingers Do the Walkin' and Talkin'!

Writing and art are good avenues for therapy with many children and adolescents. Some prefer writing or art over verbalization. Some are more proficient with writing or drawing when expressing emotions than with trying to tell someone how they feel or what they think. Therefore, as a counselor or teacher, allow the child to have a journal and ask them to write or draw two times per day. One should be done before lunch and one after lunch at a time the child chooses. If possible, have the child share with you the content or meanings of the writings/drawings in the afternoons, at first. After several sessions, change the time to have the child share in the mornings. This activity can help determine the effects of the time of day in relations to his/her stress or anxiety points.

© YouthLight, Inc.

STRATEGY #40
Finger Hugs!

Children in public places often want to cling to their caregivers (parent, grandparent, etc.). If that is not possible or appropriate (for instance, if the child is performing in a small group or alone before a crowd of people), then prior to leaving for the event the caregiver can explain why they cannot cling or hug when they arrive. Then tell the child that the love is there even when they cannot touch. Show the child how to cross his/her second finger over the index finger and explain that is the signal between the two of them that means "finger hug!" This can also be done within a school building when children are walking down the halls and want to show affection for an adult they see! (Special THANKS to Sheila Huiet for this wonderful idea!)

STRATEGY #41
I've got ROCKS in my tummy!

The facilitator or counselor needs to have available 8-10 small rocks. If this child complains of constant stomachaches, have the child name the following as you "award" the child one rock for each answer. Ask the child to place the rock on the table.

• Have you been to the doctor or told your parent that your stomach was hurting? What did they say about it?
• Where did your tummy start hurting?
• What time of day did it start hurting?
• Who were you with when it started hurting?
• How does it feel now?
• Does this happen often?
• What have you done in the past to help it feel better? Etc.

Now, exclaim, "Oh my – look at this pile of rocks! Those would be heavy in your tummy, but thank goodness you've told me enough about them to place them on the table! Let's put them in a small box or envelope and give them away!" The child will fill the box or envelope and give them back to the counselor. The counselor will then say, "Thank you very much. Your tummy may still feel a little unsettled, but at least many of your aches are in this box!"

© YouthLight, Inc.

STRATEGY #42
Clay Creations

Working with clay can be a great way to reduce anxiety and stress in children. One activity that can be used with clay involves targeting a place where the child feels anxious. If a child becomes anxious about going home, a second home- such as the house of a parent they do not live with, or school ask him/her to construct that place using clay. (Crayola Model Magic works well and is available through YouthLight catalogs.) Once the child has made a model of the place where he/she is most anxious ask questions about that place. Ask the child to tell you what he/she would like to see in that place, what would they change about it and why, what they would like to add or take away from the place, etc. Let the child explain what would make that place more relaxing.

© YouthLight, Inc.

Introduction

Thinking is a constant exercise for all children. However, thinking transferred to become useful when stressed is an exercise for all people. The cognitive exercises in this section teach children to cognitively think about strategies that can help them work through stressful situations.

STRATEGY #43
Stress Feelings – Action Chart

Have the child(ren) name his/her current stressors. Then discuss and decide on actions to be practiced. For ages 4-6 only work on 2 at a time. For the older children decide how many can be handled at once and be careful not to overload assignments. Remember this is a change of habits many times.

© YouthLight, Inc.

Stress Feelings	Action(s) (What I can do to help myself?)

© YouthLight, Inc.

STRATEGY #44
Roll With The Word Punches!

Words can hurt – and bad! When a child is called names or teased by other children it sometimes makes that child afraid to come to school. While this can be considered a form of bullying, it is not always acknowledged as such. Therefore the child being taunted must learn strategies to deal with the hurt. Teach the child(ren) that it is best to first discuss this with a trusted adult so that a definition of the action can be assessed. If, for example, it is a one time (day) situation, then the child should be taught the importance of ignoring. However, if it is a repeated situation the teacher and/or counselor should be informed so that the best action can be taken to prevent further hurtful taunting.

© YouthLight, Inc.

Roll With The Word Punches!

This activity is intended for the infrequent or common "word punches." Discuss with children the types of "word punches" and have them brainstorm ways to respond. Three examples of responses to one "word punch" are:

1) That was an easy test. You must be really dumb if you made that grade!
   (Possible response…ignore the mean statement and compliment.)
   Tell me how you did so well!

2) That was an easy test. You must be really dumb if you made that grade!
   (Possible response…be factual.)
   That hurts my feelings. "Dumb" is a mean word. Would you want someone to say that to you?

3) That was an easy test. You must be really dumb if you made that grade!
   (Possible response…change the subject and later go talk with a trusted adult or friend.)
   I saw you playing ball at recess yesterday. Have you always been a good ball player?

Have the children tell about a "word punch" they have experienced and let the other children decide on ways they might have best responded.

Word Punch

_____

_____

_____

_____

_____

_____

_____

Response

_____

_____

_____

_____

_____

_____

_____

© YouthLight, Inc.

STRATEGY #45
3 Pluses + A Wish

For some children, being corrected by a teacher embarrasses them or causes them to give up. One idea for teachers to use with over sensitive children is the 3 pluses and 1 wish strategy. With this strategy, the teacher tells the child 3 things they did well and one thing that needs improvement. For example, "I really like how you used a web to brainstorm, gave your story a title, and indented! Next time, let's work on adding details to your ideas."

STRATEGY #46
Self Talk in Class

When a child hears something that causes him/her anxiety he/she can help reduce that anxiety by using self-talk. If a child makes fun of him/her by saying "You're dumb – that's not the right answer" the child can use self talk and say "Just because I missed one question doesn't mean I'm dumb. I'll try harder next time or ask for help!" If anxiety occurs before class begins the child can begin the day by saying "I can do this! I will try my best and not give up!"

I can do that! I will not give up!

© YouthLight, Inc.

STRATEGY #47
Self Talk at Recess

Recess can often be a place where oversensitive children experience anxiety. Feelings are often hurt when a child feels like no one will play with them. Self talk such as "If no one will come over to me – I will go over to them and ask them to play" or "I will look for someone else who isn't playing with anyone and see if they want to play."

STRATEGY #48
Interview For Another View!

This strategy can be used in a small group session or given as an assignment in a one-on-one session. Work together to develop a list of questions for the child to use in an interview with another person. This strategy can help the child see that other people share the same anxieties. It can also help the child learn new ways to deal with anxieties.

© YouthLight, Inc.

What made you anxious or stressed when you were my age?_____

_____

_____

What things made you feel better?_____

_____

_____

What are things that make you anxious or stressed today? _____

_____

_____

What do you do about it? _____

_____

_____

Who do you talk to about how you feel? _____

_____

_____

How does talking about it make you feel? _____

_____

_____

Do you ever experience physical symptoms when you are anxious? _____

_____

_____

What types?_____

_____

What do you do about the symptoms? _____

_____

_____

Do you notice that your anxious feelings occur more often at a certain time of day?

_____

_____

What do you do about that? _____

_____

_____

© YouthLight, Inc.

STRATEGY #49
Tackle this test!

Tests are often a source of anxiety for school-aged children. One strategy for helping children deal with this anxiety is to teach test taking skills. Ask the child to brainstorm a list of ways he/she currently prepares for tests. Go over the list together checking the ones that are helpful. At the bottom, list strategies that need to be added in order to be a better test taker. (A good night's sleep, healthy breakfast, note cards, do not wait until the night before to study, form a study group)

STRATEGY #50
1st Things 1st!

Prioritizing is a learned skill. By teaching children and adolescents how to prioritize, it has the potential to reduce stress. Using the following example, allow the child to express what should come 1st.
- bedtime at 9:30 p.m.
- breakfast at 7:00 a.m.
- homework after school
- brushing teeth before school
- baseball practice at 8:00 p.m.
- taking out trash before leaving for school
- catching the bus to come home

Next, have the child express some things they have to accomplish or complete for the day, week, or (with older children) month. Then, allow them time to prioritize and discuss their reasoning. Show how, by breaking it down, things seem more manageable.

© YouthLight, Inc.

HOURS IN THE DAY WORKSHEET

7:30 - 9:30 AM
9:30 - 11:30 AM
11:30 AM - 1:30 PM
1:30 - 3:30 PM
3:30 - 5:30 PM
5:30 - 7:30 PM
7:30 - 9:30 PM

© YouthLight, Inc.

SUNDAY	MONDAY	TUESDAY	WEDNESDAY	THURSDAY	FRIDAY	SATURDAY

DAYS IN THE WEEK WORKSHEET

© YouthLight, Inc.

WEEKS IN THE MONTH WORKSHEET

SUNDAY	MONDAY	TUESDAY	WEDNESDAY	THURSDAY	FRIDAY	SATURDAY

© YouthLight, Inc.

STRATEGY #51

"You are never a loser until you quit trying."

-- Mike Ditka

Stress and anxiety can be reduced with children when teaching them that mistakes are a part of growing up: Ask them to interview a teacher, parent(s), teenage cousin(s), etc. and ask the following:

• Can you tell me about a bad choice you made and wished you could change it? What were you able to do to make it better?

• Has there ever been a time when both choices you had were not the ones you really wanted? Tell me how you handled it.

This activity helps children realize that even when they are not successful with the first choice, as long as they keep trying they are NOT losers!

© YouthLight, Inc.

Top Ten Reasons

10   Practice makes perfect!

9   Winners never quit and quitters never win!

8   Anything worth having is worth working for!

7   When you are at the end of the rope you can always tie a knot and hang on. — Franklin D. Roosevelt

6   Perseverance is another name for success. — Anonymous

5   Many of life's failures are people who did not realize how close they were to success when they gave up. — An Arabian Proverb

4   Keep trying. It's only from the valley that the mountain seems high. — Anonymous

3   Effort only reveals it's reward after a person refused to quit. —Napoleon Hill

2   Character consists of what you do on the third and forth tries. — John Albert Michener

1   Failure usually follows the path of least persistence. — Anonymous

Never Give Up!

© YouthLight, Inc.

STRATEGY #52
Recovering and Returning

Often when a child has been out of school for an extended illness, the return can be both physically and emotionally challenging. This can heighten anxiety. Therefore, the counselor and teacher can plan and communicate individually with the child strategies that involve the following:

- Planned rest time during the day (i.e. a visit to the counselor's office for a 15-20 minute rest break or other area depending on the school);
- A peer tutoring time to help with academic subjects that may need additional practice;
- Snack time allowed if appetite and energy has been affected;
- Extra sessions with counselor for the child to talk about his/her feelings both physically and emotionally.

STRATEGY #53

It's not WHAT you say… it's HOW you say it!

Misinterpreting another's words can be a source of stress for many children. Use this activity to show children that it's not **what** your say but **how** you say it. Provide the children with a worksheet that has several statements on it that would make another person feel bad. For instance, "You can't spell anything right," "You're not a good student," "You are so bad that no one wants to be friends with you," "You aren't good at sports." Let the children act these out with each other and discuss how they feel when someone says similar things to them. Then have the children develop "I" statements that will provide a more open line of communication. Examples of "I" statements are: "I'm worried about your grades. Would you like some help after school?" "I am sure people would want to play with you more if you made better choices about your behavior." "I see you struggling with basketball in PE. I would be glad to help you at recess."

© YouthLight, Inc.

NEGATIVE STATEMENT	POSITIVE STATEMENT
You can't spell anything right!	I have seen you helping another student in the hallway. I would like to help you practice these spelling words.
You're not a good student!	I think you can be a good student if we practice together.
You are so bad that no one wants to be friends with you!	I can tell you have a good heart. Please let it show by making good choices. Could we talk about how to improve?
You are not good at sports!	
Get out of my space!	
Move over and give me room to sit now!	
Anybody could have done that math! What's wrong with you?	
Why do you have a mean face all the time? You always look mad!	
You think you have it bad – no way so get a grip!	
You have a weird look on your face. What is wrong with you?	

© YouthLight, Inc.

STRATEGY #54
Lovin' and Leavin'

Fear of abandonment by parents is a common stressor in children. It is important to recognize this as a real fear. One important step for parents to take is to be honest with your child. If you are going to be away for several hours tell your child. Do not say general statements such as "I'll only be gone a few minutes." If possible, contact your child while you are away to ensure them that you are fine and still on schedule. Try to give your child something to look forward to when you return. You can promise to read a favorite book together or play a favorite game. Again, make sure to follow through with whatever you promise before leaving.

STRATEGY #55
Miracle Pets!

Children who have pets can relate to this activity. Have them tell you (or the small group) about their favorite pet. Allow them to describe the appearance, age, name, and other basic facts. Then ask them to share what it is that makes that pet their "favorite." Explore all the senses. Talk about the eyes, the sounds, the feel, etc. Then talk about funny things that happen with that pet.

Discuss the following with the child(ren).

• Do you feel afraid when you are with _____ (pet's name)?

• Describe how you feel when you are around _____.

• What happens when you are away from your pet and you remember all these good things?

• Explain how these feelings can help you when you are worried or anxious.

STRATEGY #56
Checking The Mind...

In the chart that follows have the child write (or describe) his/her thoughts Help the child verbalize whether these are productive (good) thoughts or non-productive (bad) thoughts. Discuss any change that might be needed to help reduce the stressful or anxious thought(s).

© Youthlight, Inc.

CHECKING THE MIND WORKSHEET

MIND'S THOUGHT	GOOD OR BAD?	NEW THOUGHT

© YouthLight, Inc.

STRATEGY #57
My Teacher and Me

This activity should be done only individually with a child. It is good if the child appears afraid or anxious about relating to his/her teacher. Allow the child to describe his/her teacher. Then have the child describe ways the teacher helps all the children. If the child has misconceptions or negative ideas, discuss the possibility of having the teacher attend the next session. If the child agrees, have him/her write down the good things (or the leader can do the writing). Then, allow the child (or leader) to write down the concerns. Schedule a session with the teacher to have the two discuss these concerns. (Any professional teacher would prefer this rather than have a child anxious about the classroom or school experience!)

STRATEGY #58
Different or Better?????

Use this activity for children who report feeling bad or anxious because they are "different." The differences could be due to physical or academic differences. The leader will help the child reframe the "differences" into positives or ways the child may be "better" in SOME areas. Concentrate on the child's talents, strengths, and positive attributes. Then discuss how everyone has strengths and weaknesses and this is nothing to be ashamed of when around others.

© YouthLight, Inc.

STRATEGY #59
Name that Attention!

Attention should be focused on the anxiety in this exercise. Name the anxious or nervous thought (or event). Talk about it in detail allowing the child to name every concern or feat that may exist. The ask, "What is the worst that can happen?" Once that has been determined by the child(ren), focus on the reality and/or possibility of the worst thought happening. Many times this will difuse any unrealistic or exaggerated thought the child has. Then reframe or give attention to the good parts of that concern and allow the child to see "both" sides!

STRATEGY #60
Change can be FUN!

Many children and adolescents experience anxiety with change. This can be as minor as a picture or piece of furniture in the bedroom being changed to a family move or change of school. It is important than the adults around this child reframe the change into positives (rather than negatives). The following worksheet can guide both the adult and child as this reframing is organized into more optimistic thoughts.

© YouthLight, Inc.

CHANGE CAN BE FUN WORKSHEET

CURRENT CHANGE BEING EXPERIENCED	NEGATIVE OR ANXIOUS THOUGHTS	LIST ANYTHING ABOUT THIS CHANGE THAT CAN BE AVOIDED	TAKE THE NEGATIVE OR ANXIOUS THOUGHT AND RESTATE IN A MORE POSITIVE WAY	ACTION PLANNED TO REMAIN MORE POSITIVE OR OPTIMISTIC ABOUT THE CHANGE

© Youthlight, Inc.

STRATEGY #61
F. L. Y. (FIND ways to LOVE YOURSELF)

When children are more confident of themselves, they are less likely to experience as many fears. In order for one to be more confident, a person needs to be at peace with self. As adults, we must help children recognize their strengths and importance. Using a picture of an airplane, discuss what is necessary for that airplane to lift off the ground and fly (designers for the airplane, mechanics, wheels for the runway, gasoline in the engine, training (for pilots and air traffic controllers), controls in the cockpit for the pilot, good weather conditions). Now talk about what it takes for the child(ren) to "F.L.Y." (FIND ways to LOVE YOURSELF). Allow time to discuss each item on the table below and have each child fill in the blank spots.

© YouthLight, Inc.

AIRPLANE	MY WAYS TO F.L.Y.
Designers for the airplane	My basic personality traits (how I was designed)…
Mechanics	What helps (fixes) me when I worry…
Wheels for the runway	What keeps me moving in the right direction (helps me stay focused)…
Gasoline in the engine	What fires me up (or gets me excited about myself)…
Training (for pilots and traffic controllers)	Things that I have learned about myself air that makes me worry less than I used to…
Controls in the cockpit pilots	What strategies (or controls) can I use for the when I start worrying or becoming anxious?
Good weather conditions	Now – practice these when I'm not worried or stressed so that I'll be in good condition when a situation arises that does cause me stress or anxiety…

© YouthLight, Inc.

STRATEGY #62

A.D.H.D.'s.
(Attitude Does Help Determine Success!)

Positive attitudes and energy go together hand in hand! When we think of A.D.H.D. in children we usually think of energy and more energy! Well, we all know that when energy is channeled in a positive direction, it can help a person achieve so very much! It is the same with positive attitudes! A positive attitude means that we look at the good parts of our current situations. Therefore, help the child(ren) experiencing stress to see the stress as a signal – maybe a warning to stop and rethink what or how they are doing the task at hand. Point out that we can be either positive (upbeat) or negative (down) but it is almost impossible to be each at the same time.

STRATEGY #63

Program My Brain!

This strategy involves self-talk techniques. Sometimes when children worry or get stressed they become unable to see anything but the negative or stressful event. When that happens, cognitively it is sometimes difficult to revert to "the good times." If "good thoughts" have been programmed into the brain, those thoughts can help when stressful times come.

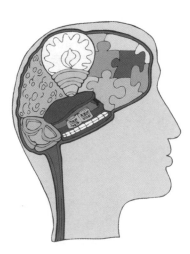

© YouthLight, Inc.

Here are some examples of thoughts to have the child practice
(of course, many more can be added to fit the specific stressful situation).

Program My Brain

• **I will be OK.**

• **This problem can only last _____ minutes (hours or days) and it will pass.**

• **Something good that I am looking forward to is**

_____.

• **I am safe because** _____.

• **_____ loves me and is always there for me.**

• **I can do well at** _____.

_____

_____

_____

_____

_____

© YouthLight, Inc.

STRATEGY #64
Smart Starts!

This helps the child who suffers from mild separation anxiety each morning. If the parent and school work together, this can encourage and motivate the child that the day will be as pleasant as possible.

- (Parent – Preferably) The night before (or the day before if the counselor or teacher needs to do so) the separation is to occur, talk with the child about his/her fears and reassure him/her that you will return. At the end of this discussion with kind, but firm words agree that tomorrow is not the time to talk, but to act – knowing that he/she will be taken care of and safe at school (or wherever the child is going).
- (Parent) At breakfast, review all the good things about yesterday. Then talk about how things can be better today! (Do not go into a dialogue as you did last night.)
- (Parent or Carpool Driver) On the ride to school sing fun, upbeat songs that require participation by those in the car (at least singing in unison).
- (Parent to Teacher at door or School Counselor) Simply give the child a hug and nod and LEAVE quickly. With mild separation anxiety, if tears occur they will disappear when the caregiver disappears (and may reoccur at night for a while).
- (Teacher / Counselor) Being very upbeat, assign the child a couple of small duties to reassure that he/she stays busy and is not sitting or standing alone at the beginning of the morning. Smile…smile….smile with the child – body language is important!
- (Teacher) At lunch and again at the end of the day, continue to be encouraging, but point the child toward more independence with other peer involvement.
- (Teacher) Provide a "last memory" – maybe a stuffed animal from the classroom that he/she can take home and bring back the next day or some special good news note for the parent(s).

STRATEGY #65
Table Time

Children feel better about themselves when they have a good relationship with their parents. Work daily at keeping the lines of communication open with your child. Question them about their day at school during dinner. Ask about the best part of their day and the worst. Let them know you care about them and that you are concerned about the things that they consider important.

© YouthLight, Inc.

STRATEGY #66
Book of Blessings

Encourage your child to focus on the positive things in life, not the negative. This can contribute to an overall feeling of well being. Let your child choose a notebook or journal and decorate the cover anyway they like. This can be a place for them to jot down all the things they are grateful for. It can be added to continuously and used as a reference when needed. If your child begins to feel sorry for themselves or complain that things never go their way remind them to look back at their book of blessings. They will be surprised to see how many things they do have to be thankful for.

STRATEGY #67
Repeat, Repeat, Repeat

Whenever a child becomes highly anxious it can help if they will repeat a calming word or phrase. Teach children phrases they can say to themselves in order to control the anxiety. Examples include: "Relax, Relax," "Stay Calm," "I'm OK," "Control, Control," etc.

STRATEGY #68
Delegate Duties

Children who are over anxious can benefit from learning how to delegate duties. They may need help realizing that their way of doing things is not the only way that can work. Working in groups at school is a great way to allow children the experience of sharing duties to get an assignment done. Not only does this help reduce anxiety but it is also a way to build friendships and trust. At home, children can work with siblings or other family members to complete chores. They will learn that the work can get done faster when everyone works together.

© YouthLight, Inc.

STRATEGY #69
Recognize Reactions

Our body has ways of letting us know when we are stressed. Children need to learn how to recognize these signs. Ask children to describe how they are feeling at times when they are over anxious. Their heart may beat fast, they may have trouble breathing, stomach aches, headaches, or nausea. Teach children to look for these signs as a signal to slow down or take a break.

STRATEGY #70
Food Facts

We are what we eat! Like adults, when children become anxious, they may tend to overeat certain types of food. Discuss with children the importance of eating healthy balanced meals and snacks. Eating the wrong types of food can lead to energy loss, which can make them less able to deal with stressful events. Check out cookbooks for children from the school or local library. Look at these with children and let them decide which recipes they would like to help prepare and sample. This is a great way to introduce children to new types of food that they would enjoy and that will be healthy for them as well.

STRATEGY #71
Who am I?

Children need to learn about themselves in order to understand who they are. This can help them see why and how they react to certain situations. Give children a copy of the worksheet "Who am I?" Allow them time to fill in their responses to the questions. Invite them to share with you their thoughts and feelings about what they discovered

© YouthLight, Inc.

I am most happy when:

_____

_____

My plans for the future are: _____

_____

_____

I like myself the best when: _____

_____

_____

I like myself the least when: _____

_____

_____

What I fear the most is: _____

_____

_____

I am disappointed when: _____

_____

_____

People would describe me as: _____

_____

_____

What I value the most is: _____

_____

_____

One negative trait I need to work on is: _____

_____

_____

One positive trait I am proud of is: _____

_____

_____

WHO AM I? WORKSHEET

© YouthLight, Inc.

STRATEGY #72
Get Focused

Assist an over anxious child in focusing his/her attention on something other than the cause of the anxiety. When a child becomes involved in something that requires focused concentration the activity is able to distract their attention. Activity suggestions include: word searches, crossword puzzles, jigsaw puzzles, card games, board games, math games, playing an instrument, or art activities.

STRATEGY #73
Lighten the Load

The demands placed on children today can sometimes prove to be too much. An over anxious child may need help lightening their load. Review your child's school and social calendar. Is he/she weighted down with social commitments, school activities, sports practice, music lessons, club meetings? Maybe some activities can wait until next year or agree on a number of activities that can be done at one time.

© YouthLight, Inc.

Introduction

When a child is tired, often anxious feelings become magnified. The ability to cope with stressful situations becomes more difficult. These strategies are designed to help the child learn to slow down and enjoy the benefits of relaxation.

STRATEGY #74
Prescription For Rest...

This activity is good for the end of the day when children are experiencing the same difficulties. However, children have less experience in how to express and control their feelings calmly. The child may cry, argue, have an outburst of anger, or simply become passive.
The leader or counselor conducting this activity should "play doctor." If possible have a white lab coat or a pretend prescription pad. Give yourself a silly name like "Dr. Sleepy Head" or "Dr. Big Snorer!" Tell the child you got that name because when you get tired you get grumpy and anxious. Talk about those feelings. Ask if he/she ever gets similar feelings.

Discuss how being tired can make us angry, sad, mad, or anxious (even scared). Think of activities that are restful (reading, listening to soft music, etc.). Then get the prescription pad and PRESCRIBE REST. Write something like, "Stretch your legs out and put your head on a pillow for 10 minutes in a quiet room (or with soft music)." "Lay down and close your eyes for 10 minutes." "Try going to bed 30 minutes earlier tonight than last night."

Have them take the "prescription" with them and come back to you for a "follow up" visit the next day. At that visit have the child describe how he/she followed your instructions. If that did not make a huge difference "prescribe" something else. Keep following up. Often the children give wonderful suggestions to each other!

© YouthLight, Inc.

Rx

Dr. _____

112 Stressfree Lane
No Street, US 90575

Prescription _____

_____

_____

_____

Extra Instructions _____

_____

_____

_____

Refills   1   2   3   4   forever

Signature _____

© YouthLight, Inc.

TOP PEST WORKSHEET

STRATEGY #75
Get your Zzzzzz's

Making sure your child's body gets the right amount of rest is very important when dealing with a stressed child. Your child's ability to deal with stressful situations will be improved with adequate sleep. Be sure to provide the child with an environment that invites peaceful sleep. Let your child help decorate their room to make it a place they feel comfortable in. Having items nearby that are important or special to the child can provide comfort. Developing a night time routine will help your child learn when it is time to begin settling down and preparing for sleep.

STRATEGY #76
Peaceful Place

Help children find a quiet place to calm down when they feel over-anxious or sensitive. In school, they may be allowed to sit quietly in the reading center with a favorite book or move their chair by the window for a few minutes. At home the child may like to sit in a special chair or in a special place. Sometimes removing themselves from the situation briefly can help them regain control.

© YouthLight, Inc.

STRATEGY #77
Work Out Wonders

When children feel over anxious or sensitive exercise can help to relax their mind and body. Any type of activity such as walking, bike riding, roller blading, skateboarding, scooter riding, or stretching can be a quick stress reliever.

STRATEGY #78
Calming Collages

Work with children in a small group or individually to make a collage on topics such as: good memories they have of a loved one who passed away, favorite things about school, relaxing pictures, people they love, pictures of favorite items from home, notes from friends and family, etc. The children can draw pictures, cut out pictures from magazines, use clip art on the computer, or paints to illustrate the collage. A file folder can be used to glue the collage onto so that it can easily fit in places like a book bag or desk at school. This will make the collage easily accessible so the child can refer to it when they are feeling anxious or stressed.

© YouthLight, Inc.

Introduction

Physical activity reduces some stress through body chemistry. The strategies in this section are popular with children. These may be helpful to use prior to relaxation or cognitive strategies with active children.

STRATEGY #79
Stress OR Stretch!

This game teaches physical relaxation in a fun way! You will need some mats (your PE teacher may be able to provide these).

Have the class members volunteer things that stress them in any location. Ask other students if they have ever experienced the same stress. For those who raise their hand in agreement, have them stretch on the mat (this will vary but be sure they really stretch). Continue this as the students discuss things that make them anxious.

After about 15 minutes, stop the game, have the children return to their desks and ask how many were helped by this exercise. Then allow discussion of whether talking or stretching was the most helpful (answers will vary). Finally, ask them to transfer this lesson and use the techniques that worked the best when they encounter a stressful situation again.

© YouthLight, Inc.

STRATEGY #80
I Don't Feel Too Good!

When anxiety is felt in various parts of the body, the child usually complains of stomach or head aches. The caregiver (parent, teacher, counselor) can reduce anxiety immediately by actively listening with understanding. Of course, as with all physical complaints, these should be medically checked first. Once it has been determined that these are not medically based but are more emotional, a "stress activity" focused on the point in the body that is hurting can be helpful. Here is how this works:

• If the palms of the hands sweat. Have the child ball his/her fists as tight as possible and count slowly to 10. Then, release the fists and feel the relaxation in the fingers! Repeat 4 more times.

• If the stomach or head hurts. Have the child tighten his/her facial muscles (make a tight face – children love this and think it is funny) and tighten his/her stomach muscles at the same time. Slowly count to 10 and release. Repeat 4 more times.

STRATEGY #81
Lap it UP!

When a "tense" time can be predicted (i.e., before school, before a ball game, before going away for the night, etc.), try to get outside or in a gym. Enjoy walking or jogging for at least 10-15 minutes while allowing the child to talk about anything on his/her mind. If outside or the gym is not possible, jog in place with the child and make a fun game out of releasing some energy and thoughts!

STRATEGY #82
Crossover (physical exercise)!

It is a well known fact that physical exercise helps stress many times in many ways! Therefore, this can be a fun activity for a child (or group of children) to release some energy and relax the body.

© YouthLight, Inc.

Crossover!

1. In a large room or outside playground label a "Start" line and measure 15 feet to label a "Finish" line. If done with an individual child the counselor needs to either participate or walk along to encourage. If done with a group of children, place one child at the finish line as the "encourager!"

2. Explain the object of the game is to get from the "Start" to the "Finish" line within 2 minutes.

3. The rules are simple. With the child facing the starting line (with his/her back to the finish line) he/she must cross legs behind the ankles while knees are bent at at 90 degree angle. Continue alternating and crossing until getting to the finish line. If the child falls, then he must run back to the starting line and start all over (with the time clock still going)!

4. At the end of the 2 minutes, if the child has completed the task, have the child describe how his/her body feels now as compared to the starting point. If the child did not complete ask him/her to try one more time!

5. Then discuss whether this task was harder or easier than the child originally thought. Why?

6. When first described, did this activity make you feel anxious at all? Why?

7. Follow with a discussion about how any new activity can be scary. However, with enough practice it gets easier.

8. End with a comparison of feelings to the current stress or anxiety the child originally experienced when he/she came to you.

ACTIVITY

© YouthLight, Inc.

STRATEGY #83
Jelly Belly

Some stress is felt in the stomach area of the body. This can have the child feel nauseated, weak, experience pain or cramps, and cause loss of (or increased) appetite. (Of course, as with any physical discomfort, medical problems should be ruled out prior to assuming these are totally emotional) If there are no medical issues noted, then the activity can focus on emotional stress. In order to combat these uncomfortable feelings, the physical activity should focus on the mid section of the body.

1. Demonstrate how to tighten the stomach muscles by breathing in and having the stomach contract into a tight knot like feeling (similar to a clinched fist).
2. Hold of 10 seconds – counting slowly.
3. Then release and wiggle the stomach without moving the other parts of the body as much as possible.
4. Repeat this 5 times.

Discuss the current feelings in the stomach. Note that even if the stomach still is uncomfortable, it probably is due to the physical exercise more than the worry now. Have the child discuss which feels worse, the emotional stress at the beginning or the physical stress after the exercise.

© YouthLight, Inc.

Introduction

Peers become extremely influential to children as they progress developmentally. The peer support strategies are great tools for ALL children – children with high social anxieties, children who tend to be more withdrawn, and children who have low self-esteem. The facilitator must be sensitive to all children participating in these activities not only the identified anxious child.

STRATEGY #84
Big Brother/Big Sister

One way to help children deal with anxiety or over sensitivity is to pair them up with an older child who may have suffered from similar problems. This will provide the child with a resource to help them deal with problems that may arise at school. Work out a schedule that works for both children to meet to discuss strategies that worked for the Big Brother or Big Sister. This may give the child something to look forward to as well – being able to help a younger child when they are older.

STRATEGY #85
Study Buddies

Encourage children to help each other study for tests! Post a sign up sheet at school for children to join study groups that can meet before or after school. The children can list what subjects they need extra help in. Divide the children into groups based on needs. Older children could help the younger children, this may be a community service project for gifted and talented classes, or any volunteers available at your school. Having a study buddy can help to reduce stress over grades and overall school achievement.

© YouthLight, Inc.

STRATEGY #86
OK Opinions

Some children and adolescents become anxious if someone disagrees with their ideas or thoughts. The result of peer pressure can be that children are afraid to express themselves. With a small group, have each person state and opinion about such things as homework, recess, lunches at school (start with easy topics) and then move into more sensitive subjects (drugs, alcohol, etc.). Encourage group members to be honest and straightforward with the understanding that no true opinion is wrong, but should be listened to and respected. At the end of this session, ask each participant what he/she learned from those expressing different opinions.

STRATEGY #87
Scavenger Hunt!

Directions: Have each child fill in the checklist/chart, which identifies his/her current fears and anxieties. Once each child has completed the checklist/chart set a timer for 5-10 minutes. Instruct the children to go on a scavenger hunt around the classroom looking for others who share the same anxiety/fears. Allow the children with similar anxiety/fears time to discuss and share.

© YouthLight, Inc.

This makes me anxious or stressed:	This is how I have handled it:	This may be a better way to handle it after talking to my friend:

© YouthLight, Inc.

STRATEGY #88
Newcomer's Club

High stress is sometimes experienced with change. Coming to a new school can affect children in various ways. For example, the child may feel he/she is the only new student. The counselor can form a "Newcomer's Club" with children who have been at the school less than a semester. The children can support each other by telling some of their experiences and how they handled them. Also, this gives the "newcomers" a group to identify with while making new friends!

STRATEGY #89
Unique Expressions

Every family or classroom is made up of unique individuals. Here is a fun family or classroom game to play that will highlight each family or class member's unique attributes. This game could also be used in a small group setting at school. Have each person make a list of several things that each family or peer member is good at. Take turns acting out each trait and letting the others guess what trait it is and what person it represents. This is a great way to celebrate differences as well as learn how special others think you are! This activity can help relieve stress in children who feel inadequate when compared to siblings or peers.

© YouthLight, Inc.

"Unique Expressions"
(charade type game)

Rules:

1 Have each family or class member make a list of several things that other family members are good at.

2 Choose a player to go first. That person will act out a trait from their list while other family members try to guess what trait it is and which family or class member it represents.

3 Keep score allowing one point per person for each correct guess. Decide ahead of time how many turns each player will get or what score you will stop at.

After the game allow time for each family or class member to share his/her thoughts.

What did they learn about how others view them?

What were they most surprised to learn about?

Where there traits that they did not realize described them?

Did the number of positive traits used to describe them surprise them?

© YouthLight, Inc.

STRATEGY #90
The Smile Challenge!

This is a great small group or classroom activity! However, if done with an individual student and the counselor, it can be relaxing as well!

Smiling is one way to help control feelings. The physical act of a smile is an uplifting and encouraging activity that anyone can do! Ask two children to volunteer to be leaders. Ask each child in the group to smile. Then ask the two leaders to stand face to face while smiling at each other. Next tell one group member to smile and say in a sad tone, "I really feel b-a-a-d" while continuing to smile. (Usually he/she will get tickled!) Then ask the other leader to say, "You really make me MAD!" while continuing to smile. You may wish to follow with some 'not so happy' statements while instructing the children to continue smiling. Allow various children to participate in this until the group appears very relaxed.

Finally, lead a discussion allowing children to explain what happened when they "made" their faces smile! Talk about the feelings of the group when this activity started as compared to how they feel now. Remind them that SMILING and JOINING OTHERS IN FUN can really help stressed or nervous feelings!

© YouthLight, Inc.

STRATEGY #91
The FRIEND game!

Have the children gather in four groups at the four corners of the classroom. (Try to plan so that the most anxious children are separated.) As the leader shares the following situations – one at a time, allow the groups to state how the situation should be handled.

1) You are with four friends on the playground. Three of the friends want to go to an area to play that is against the rules. You don't want to get into trouble, but you don't want your friends upset with you. This makes you feel anxious inside. How should this be handled?

2) Your teacher gives out a test. You are answering the questions and realize that your friends have turned in their papers and gone to the reading corner to relax. One of your friends is pointing at you and smiling. You know he/she is laughing because you are still working. You want to go be with your friends, but you don't want a bad grade on the test. What should you do to handle this?

3) This morning at breakfast your mom was upset with you because you had not done your chores the night before. She is telling you what you must do when you get home so these would be finished. You realize this will cause you to miss your soccer game. You are angry and argue with your mom. Now you are in school and wish your mom hadn't left without you telling her you were sorry. What should you do next?

Next have a child volunteer a situation with a friend, teacher, or parent that left him/her feeling anxious or stressed. Then have the groups brainstorm ways to handle these situations.

STRATEGY #92
Friendly Facts

Children who have close friendships are less at risk for developing stress and other related problems. Parents should encourage their child to make friends by scheduling play dates, sleepovers, and other fun activities. Join a sports team or church group, visit your local library for story time, anything that gives your child the opportunity to be around other children in a positive atmosphere.

© YouthLight, Inc.

STRATEGY #93
Babbling Benefits

Encourage children to find a friend or mentor who they can trust to listen without judging. Talking to another person often helps to relieve the pressure stress can cause. It can also help children find answers to their problems without someone telling them what to do. Help children find someone who is positive, up-beat, and demonstrates low stress levels.

STRATEGY #94
Healthy and Wise!

Have 4-6 students share what they do to stay healthy (example – eat well, get plenty of rest, exercise, etc.). Allow share time to talk about the last time they got anxious (example – before a test, when someone has been angry, etc.). The leader will lead a discussion on how to keep boundaries. Utilize the following discussion / question starters:

1. Describe how you feel after a good night's sleep.
2. Compare with a morning you went to sleep late or didn't sleep well.

Were nightmares or bad dreams involved? How did you feel the next morning?

3. Describe how you feel after enjoying a day playing with sisters, brothers, or friends.
4. Describe how you feel after having an argument with sisters, brothers or friends. How do you handle that (example – I worry, I cry, I get mad back, etc.)?
5. Since we are aware of different feelings, what are some things you can do to help yourself when you become anxious, stressed, or worried?

Allow children time to brainstorm and write on a board (or chart paper) as they give the ideas.

6. Discuss these ideas and ask children to copy some of these things on a sheet of paper to practice during the next week. Have them report back to the group next week some ways these ideas helped (or did not help) them cope with anxiety.

© YouthLight, Inc.

Introduction

It is important to experience appropriate humor – to lighten up on ourselves! These strategies help the child with high levels of anxiety experience some "light moments" and the value of smiling and laughing.

STRATEGY #95
Merry Mistakes!

Learning to laugh appropriately at oneself can be freeing and reduce stress significantly! As the facilitator of a small group or the counselor with an individual child use some personal experiences to show that it's all right to laugh at oneself. Examples of this could be things such as:
• When you spilled something at the dinner table accidentally;
• When you tripped over your own foot and almost dropped something valuable;
• When you used an incorrect word by mistake; etc.
Ask the child to share a time he/she was embarrassed and help him/her reframe it into a "Merry Mistake."

STRATEGY #96
Learn to Laugh

Laughter can be the best medicine for stress! There has been a lot of research done to show the benefits of laughing and smiling. Share with children the joy of a good laugh. Read joke books, humorous poetry, funny stories, or cartoons. Try to schedule a couple of laugh breaks throughout the school day. When changing from one activity to another read a quick joke or share a funny cartoon on the overhead. Moments like these can help children release stress, forget their worries, and relax.

© YouthLight, Inc.

STRATEGY #97
Shout And Squeal!

This activity should be done outside and is great for a small group of about 5 children. In the format of a game, have the children stand in a circle. Have the children decide or ask for a volunteer to stand in the middle. Ask the middle child to name one thing he/she is afraid of (i.e. tests, snakes, etc.). Then, ask each child one by one standing in the circle to name a way the middle child could conquer that fear. If the middle child likes the idea he is supposed to "shout and squeal." Then the child offering the suggestion gets in the center of the circle and starts the process again. This not only adds laughter to the game, good suggestions are shared! The leader should then discuss with the children how helpful it is to share anxious feelings and fears with others in order to hear ways to help conquer those fears.

STRATEGY #98
Scream Sack
(From the "Chill Out" bag by Youthlight, Inc.)

This activity should be done outside or in a physical education room. Using the "Chill Out" bag (www.youthlightbooks.com) "Scream Sack", share with the child something that makes you nervous or frustrated (example, meeting a time limit with your work). Then, you scream into the sack until it blows up! Next, have the child name a stressful or anxious situation that makes them feel nervous or frustrated. Allow them to open the sack and scream into it until it blows out and is filled with air. Then have the child talk about this situation and how it felt to scream!

© YouthLight, Inc.

STRATEGY #99

Laughing Bag!

(From the "Chill Out" bag by Youthlight, Inc.)

Have the child tell you about his/her day (both positives and negatives). Ask the following questions for discussion:

- After you began getting ready for school, what things were on your mind as you got dressed?
- Were any thoughts on your mind that made you feel nervous or anxious? If so, name those thoughts.
- Has the day been better than you thought so far? If not, what has happened?

Next, help the child reframe some positive thoughts about the remainder of his/her day and share how attitudes can help us overcome some of our anxious thoughts. Talk about the act of smiling and practice with the child the feelings of a smile on your face! Finally, give the child the "Laughing Bag" and have him/her squeeze the bag. Watch the reaction and laugh with the child! Continue several times. Then, discuss how talking, smiling, and laughing can help us feel less stressed.

© Youthlight, Inc.

STRATEGY #100
Stress Cards!

Get a laundry bag and write (with a permanent marker) STRESS on the outside in large letters! Give each child five (5) index cards (any size). Have each child write (with a pen or regular marker) one thing that makes them anxious or stressed on each index card and drop those in the laundry bag. Then proceed with a discussion while putting the laundry bag in the corner of the room.

Tell the child(ren) you will meet with them tomorrow to learn more about ways to handle stresses -- and to find out what happens to the index cards when stress is handled! (This adds a little mystery to the activity.)

The counselor (or leader) will then take the index cards and soak them in clear water for 2 minutes. Lay them out to dry (or put them in a hosiery bag to dry in your dryer at home). The next day, place these back into the laundry bag.

Meet with the children and ask a child to draw out a "Stress Card." The children will wonder what has happened. Have another child do the same and continue until the cards have been drawn. See if any of the stresses can be read. If the card is readable, talk about how it "changed." If it is not readable, talk about how it has "disappeared." Then discuss how stresses change or disappear sometimes after we talk about them.

© YouthLight, Inc.

STRATEGY #101
TIPS FOR PARENTS

- Keep in mind that certain levels of worry or anxiety are normal in children. Anxiety can help children be alert to their surroundings.
- Be aware that the fears of your child are very real to him/her. It is important to acknowledge your understanding of that fear. Encourage your child to talk about the anxiety with you and provide comfort as this anxiety is discussed.
- Seek professional help when you feel like your child's anxiety is interfering with their everyday life.
- Make an effort to always be truthful and calm when speaking with your child. Anxiety can be contagious so be a good role model of how to properly manage your feelings.
- Don't go through this alone. There are many resources available to assist you in helping your anxious or stressed child.
- Realize that you can't be everything to your child. It is alright to seek assistance through others to help your child with their anxiety or stress.
- Avoid discussing topics that you are anxious about in front of your child such as finances or marital problems. These are issues that your child cannot fix so they should not be burdened with worry over them.
- Let your child know how you can be reached in case of emergencies.
- Be alert to what your child is viewing through the media. News of wars, violence, natural disasters, etc. can be traumatic to your child.
- Remember to practice active listening to learn how your child is defining his/her fear.
- Help your child to enjoy physical activities as a way to reduce anxiety and stress.
- Recognize your child's talents and strengths in order to encourage success. Feeling successful can lead to feelings of self-worth.

© YouthLight, Inc.

References

Frank, K., (2003), *The Handbook for Helping Kids With Anxiety & Stress,* YouthLight, Inc., Chapin, SC.

Martin, Michael & Waltman-Greenwood, Cynthia, (1995), *Solve Your Child's School-Related Problems,* The Philip Lief Group, Inc. and the National Association of School Psychologists, New York.

Schachter, Dr. Robert, and McCauley, Carole Spearin, (1988), *When Your Child Is Afraid,* Simon & Schuster Inc., New York.

Steiner, Hans, (1997), *Treating School-Age Children,* Jossey-Bass Publishers, San Francisco, CA.

Turecki, Stanley, and Wernick, Sarah, (1994), *Normal Children Have Problems, Too,* Bantam Books, New York.

© YouthLight, Inc.

Appendix A:

Criteria For Generalized Anxiety Disorder
(Includes Overanxious Disorder of Childhood)

There must be an excessive amount of worry and anxious anticipation that is difficult to manage or control for a minimum of 6 months. Generalized Anxiety Disorder should be diagnosed utilizing a thorough evaluation by a medical or licensed mental health professional so that this is not over diagnosed in children. According to the DSM-IV-TR the symptoms of this condition can appear similar to *Separation Anxiety Disorder, Social Phobia, and Obsessive-Compulsive Disorder.*

Generalized Anxiety Disorder

- Excessive worry and anxiety for most days lasting at least 6 months about activities in various locations (i.e., school, social, work, etc.).
- The worry is not easy to control.
- One of the following should be present (in children):
    - restlessness or being on edge
    - tiring easily
    - hard to concentrate or blanks out material
    - irritability
    - tension in muscles
    - difficulty sleeping (either falling or staying asleep, or waking tired from a restless sleep)
- The worry and/or anxiety is not related to embarrassment, panic, being separated from relatives or loved ones, weight fluctuations, numerous physical complaints, an acute sickness, or the result of a traumatic event.
- There is excessive impairment in significant and important areas of functioning such as school, social interactions, work, etc.
- The impairment is not due to medication, illegal drugs, a medical condition, Pervasive Developmental Disorder, or a Psychotic Disorder.

From American Psychiatric Association (2000). *Diagnostic and statistical manual of mental disorders, fourth edition, text revision,* Washington, DC. (pp. 472-476)

© YouthLight, Inc.

Appendix B:

Criteria for Separation Anxiety Disorder

This diagnosis is only given if, for a minimum of at least 4 weeks and prior to age 18, there is excessive anxiety due to being separated from the home or a major attachment figure in the child's life (i.e., parent, grandparent, sibling, etc.). An early onset is noted if this occurs before a child is age 6.

Separation Anxiety Disorder
- Three (3) or more of the following must be present and must be developmentally inappropriate with extreme anxiety.
    * Persistent major distress when worrying about being separated from home or a major attachment figure(s).
    * Extreme and continuing fear that someone close will be harmed, hurt, or die.
    * Extreme and continuing worry concerning a possible traumatic event (i.e., being lost or kidnapped).
    * Extreme and continuing fear of being separated that results in refusal to go to school and other places.
    * Acute and excessive reluctance, due to fears, of being alone and without either attachment figures or familiar adults at home or in other settings.
    * Continuing refusal or extreme reluctance to spend the night away from home or to go to sleep without a major attachment figure.
    * Recurring nightmares related to separation fears.
    * Frequent physical complaints (i.e., headaches, stomach aches, nausea, vomiting, etc.) that are not due to a medical condition.
- The significant anxiety must last at least 4 weeks.
- It must start before a child is 18 years old.
- The distress or lack of ability to function in academic, social, or other important areas of functioning must be severe.
- The trouble must not exist exclusively due to Panic Disorder with Agoraphobia, Pervasive Developmental Disorder, or other Psychotic conditions.

From American Psychiatric Association (2000). *Diagnostic and statistical manual of mental disorders, fourth edition, text revision,* Washington, DC. (pp. 121-125).

© YouthLight, Inc.

Appendix C:

Recommended Resources on Anxiety in Children and Related Topics

The following related resources can be ordered through YouthLight, Inc.
P. O. Box 115, Chapin, SC 29036
1-800-209-9774 Telephone
1-803-345-0888 FAX
Email yl@sc.rr.com
www.youthlight.com

Allen, J. & Klein, R. (1996). *Ready…Set…R.E.L.A.X.: A Research Based Program of Relaxation, Learning, and Self Esteem for Children.* Inner Coaching.

Cave, K. (2003). *You've Got Dragons.* Peachtree Publishers, L.T.D.

Crist, J. (2004). *What to Do When You're Scared and Worried.* Free Spirit Publishing.

Frank, K. (2003). *The Handbook for Helping Kids With Anxiety & Stress.* YouthLight, Inc.

Goodwin, J. (2005). Mustang, *The Little Dog Who Was Afraid to Go to School.* YouthLight, Inc.

Kuczen, B. & Kuczen, C. (1999). *Pass-Along Papers: 52 Parent Handouts Ready to Photocopy and Pass-Along!!!* Active Parenting Publishers.

Moritz, K. & Jablonsky, J. (1998). *Blink, Blink, Clop, Clop: Who Do We Do Things We Can't Stop?* Childswork/Childsplay.

Niner, H. (2004). *Mr. Worry: A Story About OCD.* Albert Whitman & Co.

Oehlberg, B. (1996). *Making It Better: Activities for Children Living in a Stressful World.* Redleaf Press.

Romain, T. & Verdick, E. (2000). *Stress Can Really Get on Your Nerves.* Free Spirit Publishing.

Shuman, C. (2003). *Jenny is Scared! When Sad Things Happen in the World.* Magination Press.

Waltz, M. (2000). *Obsessive-Compulsive Disorder: Help for Children and Adolescents.* O'Reilly & Associates, Inc.

© YouthLight, Inc.

Other Resources

Fitzgibbons, L. & Pedrick, C. (2003). *Helping Your Child With OCD: A Workbook for Parents of Children with Obsessive-Compulsive Disorder.* Oakland, CA: New Harbinger Publications, Inc.

Rapee, R., Spence, S., Cobham, V., & Wignall, A. (2000). *Helping Your Anxious Child: A Step-by-Step Guide for Parents.* Oakland, CA: New Harbinger Publications, Inc.

Rapee, R., Wignall, A., Hudson, J., & Schniering. (2000). *Treating Anxious Children and Adolescents: An Evidence-Based Approach.* Oakland, CA: New Harbinger Publications, Inc.

© YouthLight, Inc.